S T O P !

READ THE GOOD NEWS

Thirty-One Scriptures That Can Touch,
Motivate and Change Your Life

LOU SLAUTTERBACK

CROSSBOOKS
PUBLISHING

CrossBooks™
A Division of LifeWay
1663 Liberty Drive
Bloomington, IN 47403
www.crossbooks.com
Phone: 1-866-879-0502

First published by CrossBooks 4/26/2012

ISBN: 978-1-4627-1534-3 (e)
ISBN: 978-1-4627-1535-0 (sc)

Library of Congress Control Number: 2012906234

Printed in the United States of America

This book is printed on acid-free paper.

CONTENTS

Introduction vii

Dedication... xi

Acknowledgments xv

Selection 1: God's Perfect Plan 1

Selection 2: God's Word Is Alive 2

Selection 3: God Loves Me 3

Selection 4: I Am a Sinner.. 4

Selection 5: Christ Died for Me 5

Selection 6: One Way 6

Selection 7: God Knocked on My Heart's Door 7

Selection 8: God Wants All My Love 8

Selection 9: Wonderfully Made.. 9

Selection 10: This Is a Special Day.................................... 10

Selection 11: Who Do You Work For? 11

Selection 12: Balanced Living... 12

Selection 13: Perfect Peace 13

Selection 14: Decision Time.. 14

Selection 15: Hope in the Lord 15

Selection 16: Trust in the Lord 16

Selection 17: Jesus Is Always There 21

Selection 18: Be Strong and Stand Firm 22

Selection 19: Keep the Sabbath 23

Selection 20: Self-Examination... 24

Selection 21: Do Not Follow the Crowd............................. 25

Selection 22: Read the Word, Get Blessed 26

Selection 23: I Can Know I Have Eternal Life.................................... 27

Selection 24: My Witness 29

Selection 25: The Cardinal 30

Selection 26: Hope in Jesus 32

Selection 27: Love, the Greatest of These 33

Selection 28: Gift of God... 34

Selection 29: Who is Jesus? 35

Selection 30: Have Faith: God Will Take Care of You 36

Selection 31: A Perfect Prayer.. 37

Final Thought.. 39

For Further Reading... 41

INTRODUCTION

I am thankful for the good news I read daily in God's holy Word. I was raised in a Christian family and nurtured in the church. Sunday school and weekly worship were not an option in my home: you were going to attend regardless of any reluctance you might be experiencing. I am thankful for that guidance and upbringing. I also had the fortune to be surrounded by loving and caring Christian parents, relatives, parishioners, and clergy who cultivated, encouraged, and facilitated my faith.

Regardless of my background, I had to make the personal decision to invite Jesus into my life. I was very young; the experience occurred at my country church in Kittanning, Pennsylvania. I am uncertain who preached on that particular day, but I knew Jesus was knocking on my heart's door, and I had to decide what exactly I would do with the encounter. I made the right choice when I asked Jesus to come into my heart and life.

Through the years, I have had many ups and downs, but one thing I am very certain: My faith in the Lord Jesus remains secure. I stand on the Word of God and trust the Lord completely in my life. My God is bigger than any shortcoming I might have or will face. I know God has blessed my life in so many ways: a loving family; compassionate and trustworthy friends; a knowledgeable and Bible-believing church lineage; a fulfilling and stable career; and most important, the hope of eternal life in God's kingdom.

While presenting at a student leadership conference for the health, physical education, recreation, and dance profession, I was approached by two of the participants. "Mr. Slautterback we really enjoyed your talk this morning and wanted to know if we could sit and talk about your faith," said the young men.

I had been the second presenter at the conference on a beautiful fall morning. My talk, "Be Motivated—Be Enthusiastic—Be Prepared—Be a LEADER!" included ten key characteristics that I believe great leaders possessed. My first point was balanced living. I believe great leaders approach life and its challenges from a balanced approach. Mentally, physically, socially, emotionally, and spiritually, great leaders keep their lives in balance. I told the college students that while most students were very adept in the social dimension, many often minimize the other dimensions. I also shared that my faith was a priority.

My priorities are faith, family, friends, and work. As a committed Christian, I feel compelled to write a Christian devotional that could help those who inquire about my faith. The legacy I leave when I depart this world is far too important in the kingdom work of God than any other goal I may attain or realize. I don't want or desire anything less than what God intends for my life. As I share my faith through a devotional format, it is my desire to help those who are lost to find the love, forgiveness, and grace of the Savior.

It is my plan to share the good news in what I call STOP format. Please review the basic outline for each Scripture selection:

S (Scripture)

T (Thought/Think about it)

O (Outline Priority)

P (Prayer)

Stop and Take a Moment to Reflect:

Suggested Reading:

The Scripture, thought, priority, and prayer stem from my background and walk with God. The moment to reflect presents an opportunity for the reader to consider the Bible selection in his or her faith walk. In my own life, I know that I never want to leave my home and face the challenges of the day without taking time to read the Word and prayerfully seek God's will for my life. I am not so presumptuous as to believe my writing is more important than any other; I am compelled to share my thoughts in the hope that I can lead someone into an eternal relationship with my Savior. God has blessed me with the privilege of helping several people find Jesus. I hope to help others experience the same opportunity.

My prayer: Dear Jesus, bless each person as he or she reads through this short devotional. I trust you to touch his or her heart with the verses from your inspired holy Word. May the Holy Spirit enlighten, challenge, and lead the reader into a renewed relationship with God. I pray this in the blessed and holy name of God the Father, God the Son, and God the Holy Spirit. Amen.

DEDICATION

"Scotty"

In the spring of 1959, my family relocated to Baldwin, a community in the south hills of Pittsburgh. That move would prove to be a blessing in my life.

At the time of the relocation, I was thirteen years old and in the eighth grade. Our home was situated on a well-manicured corner lot and included many wonderful amenities. My dad put in the best topsoil and strategically planted shrubs and trees, which enhanced the appearance and appeal of the neighborhood.

Shortly after we moved in, we met our neighbors. The home adjacent to ours was the Harold Eugene Scott home. Scotty, as many called him, was placed in my life at a time when I would absolutely need him the most. He and his family owned a feed store that had been in their family for over one hundred years. Although short in stature, he was a giant in terms of living life.

Scotty made the commute to the feed store daily, heartily greeting the many customers who had sought his wares for generations. On several occasions, he asked if I could come and help unload a boxcar load of dog chow, monkey chow, or various other items that were too numerous to recall. The F. W. Scott Company supplied products not only to the local consumers but also to the nearby Pittsburgh Zoo and the University of Pittsburgh. Scotty's mother and brother Walter welcomed my contributions to the tasks that needed additional labor. The energy and sweat put into the undertaking was fundamental in my adolescent development.

Throughout my youth and young adulthood, Scotty and his family became a wholesome part of my life. I loved being with his wife, Melva, and the children, Gary, Mark, and Cindy. I often climbed in the sandbox or the inflatable swimming pool with his children and enjoyed their energy and youthful exuberance. As the years went by, the family embraced our relationship, and I spent increased time in their presence.

As I went off to college, I missed their family as much as my own and welcomed the chance to return home for a weekend, which frequently included some type of interaction with the Scott family. We did so many enjoyable things together; frequent trips to the beach, backyard pool engagements, holiday celebrations, picnics, dinners, amusement parks, and the annual Brentwood parade all became a meaningful and desirable part of my life.

As the years rapidly passed, Scotty supported me in every possible way. I was honored to have him serve as an usher in my wedding. Little did I know back in 1959 how much Scotty and his family would enhance my daily life and the life of my future family. Even though I relocated after college graduation, the entire Scott family continues to be an integral part of my family to this day. I no longer consider the Scotts friends; they are family.

Scotty's life was too short. His health deteriorated quickly, and before I knew it, he was gone. Looking back, I treasure the moments we spent together in laughter, work, and genuine love and friendship. I remember telling Scotty, "I don't just want to know you here on Earth; I want to know you for eternity." He assured me that he had made his peace with God and that we would see each other in heaven. We prayed together the day I inquired about his personal relationship with God.

I desire to know all my friends and family not just for the short time I live on this planet, but for eternity. I know God has a perfect plan for my life and for yours. This devotional is my attempt to help assure you that our relationship will last forever.

I dedicate this short devotional to my friend, Harold Eugene "Scotty" Scott and to his family, who has embraced and loved my family unconditionally since my youth.

Mark 12:30-31 King James Version (KJV)

"And thou shalt love the Lord thy God with all thy heart, and with all thy soul, and with all thy mind, and with all thy strength: this is the first commandment. And the second is like, namely this, Thou shalt love thy neighbor as thyself. There is none other commandment greater than these."

Mark 12:30-31 New International Version (NIV)

"Love the Lord your God with all your heart and with all your soul and with all your mind and with all your strength. The second is this: Love your neighbor as yourself. There is no commandment greater than these."

ACKNOWLEDGMENTS

Readers and Reviewers:

Susan Slautterback (My wife)

Bethany Slautterback (My daughter)

Julie Scott (Friend)

Rev. Ken Lyle (My cousin from Texas)

Rev. Edwin Deuschle (My cousin from Mississippi)

Rev. David Janz (My pastor, Christ United Methodist Church, Franklin PA)

David and Betsy Updegrave (Christian friends and fellow parishioners)

Scott and Debbie Walters (Christian friends and fellow parishioners)

Editor:

Merrill Cowart (Neighbor, Colleague, Advisor and Friend— St. John's Episcopal Church, Franklin, Pennsylvania)

Ministers:

Rev. Henry Miller (Union Baptist Church, Kittanning, Pennsylvania)

Rev. William Gust (Grace Baptist, Pittsburgh, Pennsylvania)

Rev. Alan Oyer (West Mifflin Community Baptist, Pittsburgh, Pennsylvania)

Rev. John Peterson (Center Presbyterian Church, Slippery Rock, Pennsylvania)

Rev. John Harrington (First Baptist Church, Franklin, Pennsylvania)

Rev. John Sass (Christ United Methodist Church, Franklin, Pennsylvania)

Rev. Ralph Tanner (Ambassador for Christ, Franklin, Pennsylvania)

Rev. David Holste (Christ United Methodist Church, Franklin, Pennsylvania)

Rev. Ken Peters (Christ United Methodist Church, Franklin, Pennsylvania)

Rev. Sam Wagner (My Pastor, Christ United Methodist Church, Franklin, Pennsylvania)

Rev. David Janz (My pastor, Christ United Methodist Church, Franklin, Pennsylvania)

SELECTION 1: **GOD'S PERFECT PLAN**

S (Scripture) Jeremiah 29:11: "'For I know the plans I have for you,' declares the LORD, 'plans to prosper you and not to harm you, plans to give you hope and a future.'"

T (Thought/Think about it) God loves me! God has a plan for my life!

O (Outline Priority) I know the truth of this verse. I have personally experienced his love and plan for my life. I gave myself to Jesus at a young age. The Lord has directed and helped me to fulfill his perfect plan. I am not perfect by any means. However, my God has kept me in the palm of his hand. His plan is the best plan.

P (Prayer) Lord God, thank you for reaching out to me. I trust in you and the truth of your Word. I pray my actions, words, and deeds will bring honor and glory to your holy name. My future—yes, my hope—rests in the knowledge of personally knowing you, my Lord and Savior. Amen.

Stop and Take a Moment to Reflect: Do you know and understand that God loves you and has the perfect plan for your life?

Suggested Reading: Jeremiah 29: 4 - 14

SELECTION 2: **GOD'S WORD IS ALIVE**

S (Scripture) Hebrews 4:12: "For the word of God is alive and active. Sharper than any double-edged sword, it penetrates even to dividing soul and spirit, joints and marrow; it judges the thoughts and attitudes of the heart."

T (Thought/Think about it) God's Word is living. It is active and sharp; it penetrates my soul and judges my thoughts, my actions, and my heart.

O (Outline Priority) As I read God's Word, may it cut into my thoughts, my sin, my guilt, my joys, my sorrows, and my triumphs. As I live my life, may the Word of God be my ultimate guide.

P (Prayer) Thank you, Lord, for the Bible. I love to read, study, and contemplate its wisdom, guidance, and knowledge. I stand on the Word of God; may it guide my life and my path. Thank you, Lord, for your will revealed to me daily through the reading of the Word. I trust you, love you, and treasure your Word. Help me, Lord, to share your truth with those who lack knowledge and wisdom of the living Word. Amen.

Stop and Take a Moment to Reflect: Have you read the world's best seller lately?

Suggested Reading: Hebrews 4:1-13

SELECTION 3: **GOD LOVES ME**

S (Scripture) John 3:16: "For God so loved the world that he gave his one and only Son, that whoever believes in him shall not perish but have eternal life."

T (Thought/Think about it) God loved me so much that he gave his Son that I might have life eternal!

O (Outline Priority) I believe and accept the love of God expressed to me in the best gift ever given, Jesus Christ.

P (Prayer) Lord God, I accept Jesus as my personal Savior. In Jesus' name. Amen.

Stop and Take a Moment to Reflect: Have you ever accepted Jesus Christ as your personal Savior? If not, I urge you today to confess your sins and accept the grace and forgiveness of Jesus, the Christ. I encourage you to pray this simple prayer: "Lord God, I confess I am a sinner and have need of your love, grace, and forgiveness. Dear Jesus, come into my heart and stay there forever. I pray in your holy name. Amen."

Suggested Reading: John 3:1-18

SELECTION 4: **I AM A SINNER**

S (Scripture) Romans 3:23: "All have sinned and fall short of the glory of God."

T (Thought/Think about it) No one has to tell me that I am a sinner. I sin in spite of myself. I was born a sinner, and every day, sin entices me. My thoughts, actions, and attitudes are often less than I would like them to be.

O (Outline Priority) I admit it; I am a sinner and fall short of the glory of God.

P (Prayer) Lord Jesus, thank you for loving me enough to come to Earth so that I may have a restored relationship with God. Sin makes sense to me, so I stand in need of the love and grace of a Savior. In Jesus' name. Amen.

Stop and Take a Moment to Reflect: Despite the popular worldview, there will be a day of accountability. I want to have Jesus standing beside me when that day arrives.

Suggested Reading: Romans 3:21-31

SELECTION 5: **CHRIST DIED FOR ME**

S (Scripture) Romans 5:8: "God demonstrates His own love toward us, in that while we were yet sinners, Christ died for us."

T (Thought/Think about it) God loves me in spite of my sin. He loves me so much that He sent His only Son to die for me.

O (Outline Priority) I accept the love of God my Father and the grace and forgiveness of Jesus' death on the cross.

P (Prayer) Wonderful God, I did not deserve the sacrifice so freely given for my salvation. I praise your holy name today and all days for your love and grace. In Jesus' name. Amen.

Stop and Take a Moment to Reflect: There's a song that says, "He could have called ten thousand angels." God did not. Think about his love for you and me.

Suggested Reading: Romans 5:1-11

SELECTION 6: **ONE WAY**

S (Scripture) John 14:6: "Jesus said to him, 'I am the way, and the truth, and the life, no one comes to the Father but through me.'"

T (Thought/Think about it) There is no other way to eternal life in heaven except through Jesus Christ. It is very clear to me; being good is not good enough! I cannot earn my way to heaven. It is a free gift!

O (Outline Priority) I believe in Jesus as the only way, the only truth, and the only life connection to God the Father.

P (Prayer) Jesus, thank you for the simplicity of this message. I believe you alone. In Jesus' name. Amen.

Stop and Take a Moment to Reflect: The truth of God's Word has always been foremost in my thinking. What about you?

Suggested Reading: John 14:1-14

SELECTION 7: **GOD KNOCKED ON MY HEART'S DOOR**

S (Scripture) Revelation 3:20: "Behold, I stand at the door and knock; if anyone hears My voice and opens the door, I will come in to him."

T (Thought/Think about it) I was a young boy when I felt your knock at my heart's door.

O (Outline Priority) As a child, the knock on my heart's door was evident. I responded and asked you to enter my heart. At that moment, you came into my heart, my life, and my eternity.

P (Prayer) Lord Jesus Christ, thank you for knocking on my heart's door. I know you have guided and directed my every step since that moment. In spite of myself, you have stayed in my heart. Forgive me for those moments when I failed and let you down. Thank God, you have inhabited my heart, my life, my good moments, and my disappointing moments. How blessed I am. In Jesus' name. Amen.

Stop and Take a Moment to Reflect: Have you ever felt God knocking on your heart's door?

Suggested Reading: Revelation 3:14-22

SELECTION 8: **GOD WANTS ALL MY LOVE**

S (Scripture) Mark 12:30-31 KJV: "And thou shalt love the Lord thy God with all thy heart, and with all thy soul, and with all thy mind, and with all thy strength: this is the first commandment. And the second is like, namely this, Thou shalt love thy neighbour as thyself. There is none other commandment greater than these."

T (Thought/Think about it) Scripture states that we are to love the Lord completely. It also declares we are to love our neighbor completely.

O (Outline Priority) I need my heart, soul, mind, and strength to be in complete control of and submission to the Lord of life.

P (Prayer) Lord, help me, I pray, to follow the commandments of your holy Word. Thank you for the grace that covers my shortcomings. In the name of Jesus. Amen.

Stop and Take a Moment to Reflect: God doesn't want second place in my heart. He wants to be first. God also wants me to reach out completely to my neighbor, whoever that might be.

Suggested Reading: Mark 12:28-34

SELECTION 9: **WONDERFULLY MADE**

S (Scripture) Psalm 139:13-14: "For you created my inmost being; you knit me together in my mother's womb. I praise you because I am fearfully and wonderfully made; your works are wonderful, I know that full well."

T (Thought/Think about it) God knew me before my birth. He knew the days of my life, beginning and end. He knew the plans he had for my life.

O (Outline Priority) These two verses were my mother's favorite Bible verses. Praise the Lord for these words of promise and hope. I know God created me for a specific purpose, and I will seek to live out His purpose for my life daily.

P (Prayer) Lord, please tell me daily where I should go, what I should say, to whom I should say it, and how I should react to certain situations. You know my days before they come into being. Help me, Lord, to be all that you have planned for me to be. I don't want to step left or right of your perfect plan for my life. I pray for forgiveness when I have failed you, Lord of my life. Keep me on the perfect path that I may help others to know your love and plan for their lives. Amen.

Stop and Take a Moment to Reflect: How amazing that God knew you before your birth? God made you and me!

Suggested Reading: Psalm 139

SELECTION 10: **THIS IS A SPECIAL DAY**

S (Scripture) Psalm 118:24 KJV: "This is the day which the LORD hath made; we will rejoice and be glad in it."

T (Thought/Think about it) Each day is a gift from God.

O (Outline Priority) I will rejoice in each day the Lord gives me life.

P (Prayer) Father God, thank you for life. Help me, I pray, not to complain or talk negatively. Help me to rejoice in each day you have made. Help me to see your hand in each and every moment. I pray that I can be a source of strength and hope for those who need a lift. I desire to share your light, power, and wisdom with those who need to know the truth of your holy Word. Thank you, Lord, for this day; I will rejoice and be glad in it. Praise your holy name. Amen.

Stop and Take a Moment to Reflect: Have you rejoiced today?

Suggested Reading: Psalm 118

SELECTION 11: **WHO DO YOU WORK FOR?**

S (Scripture) Colossians 3:23: "Whatever you do, work at it with all your heart, as working for the Lord, not for human masters."

T (Thought/Think about it) Since I work for the Lord, I need to give my all, my very best, my everything so that, regardless of what may happen to me or in my relationship with others, the Lord's will for my life will prevail.

O (Outline Priority) The verse is clear: I don't work for men, I work for the Lord. I gave my heart completely to the Lord; God the Father, God the Son, and God the Holy Spirit will decide what, when, and where my work will be.

P (Prayer) Lord God, I praise your holy name for all you have done in my life. My family, my friends, my church, my work are all a result of your will for my life. I fear no one. You are on the throne of my life, and I feel your hand, your spirit encouraging and directing every step. I trust you completely and praise your holy name. Amen.

Stop and Take a Moment to Reflect: When the work is difficult, remember it is God you work for, not man.

Suggested Reading: Colossians 3

SELECTION 12: **BALANCED LIVING**

S (Scripture) Luke 2:52: "And Jesus grew in wisdom and stature, and in favor with God and man."

T (Thought/Think about it) Jesus led a balanced life, mentally, physically, spiritually, and socially.

O (Outline Priority) I will strive to live a balanced life.

P (Prayer) Lord God, help me each day to achieve balance in my life in order that I may fulfill your perfect plan for my life. I seek to do your will, and in order to accomplish that goal, I must strike the balance every day. Amen.

Stop and Take a Moment to Reflect: What part of my life needs balance?

Suggested Reading: Luke 2:41–52

SELECTION 13: **PERFECT PEACE**

S (Scripture) Isaiah 26:3 "You will keep in perfect peace him whose mind is steadfast, because he trusts in you."

T (Thought/Think about it) Who would not want a peaceful life?

O (Outline Priority) My trust and faith are in the Lord Jesus Christ.

P (Prayer) Jesus, thank you for the peace I have experienced in my life. I trust you completely. Amen.

Stop and Take a Moment to Reflect: Daily, the newspapers report chaos, disorder, and pandemonium. Fortunately, I have a God who will keep my mind at peace amid the bedlam and confusion of humanity. Do you want to experience God's peace? Trust him completely.

Suggested Reading: Isaiah 26

SELECTION 14: **DECISION TIME**

S (Scripture) John 1:12: "As many as received Him, to them He gave the right to become children of God, even to those who believe in His name."

T (Thought/Think about it) I have a decision to make. The most important decision I will ever make is to receive Jesus or to reject Jesus. That is the most important choice I will encounter!

O (Outline Priority) I choose Jesus today, tomorrow, and forever.

P (Prayer) Lord Jesus, I receive you into my heart and life. In your name. Amen.

Stop and Take a Moment to Reflect: Believe and receive are both in John 1:12. To believe in Jesus is one thing, to receive the love, grace, and forgiveness he provides is quite another. Do you believe and receive the greatest gift ever given?

Suggested Reading: John 1:1-18

SELECTION 15: **HOPE IN THE LORD**

S (Scripture) Job 19:25: "I know that my Redeemer lives, and that in the end he will stand upon the earth."

T (Thought/Think about it) Despite all that Job experienced, he still placed his hope in the Lord. This verse is my wife Susan's favorite verse.

O (Outline Priority) Regardless of any trial I have or will experience, my faith, my hope, my joy is in the Lord.

P (Prayer) Lord Jesus, I trust you now, and I will trust you always. In your name. Amen.

Stop and Take a Moment to Reflect: In the end, Jesus is the only thing that will truly matter.

Suggested Reading: Job 19

SELECTION 16: **TRUST IN THE LORD**

S (Scripture) Proverbs 3:5-6: "Trust in the LORD with all your heart and lean not on your own understanding; in all your ways submit to him, and he will make your paths straight."

T (Thought/Think about it) These two verses are my favorite verses in the Bible. They have helped me through some of the most difficult trials and struggles of my life and have worked miracles in my heart, bringing healing, peace, and hope during challenging periods.

O (Outline Priority) I am determined to trust the Lord with all my heart.

P (Prayer) Oh Lord my God, thank you for these two verses, which have great impact and meaning to me. I praise and glorify your holy Word that brings healing to my heart, soul, and mind. I love you, Lord. Amen.

Stop and Take a Moment to Reflect: Have you learned to trust the Lord with all your heart?

Suggested Reading: Proverbs 3

Lou Slautterback 1948—Kittanning, Pennsylvania

Lou's Parents: Arthur and Jane; Sisters: Gladys and Marion;
and Brother: Fred—and Lou—1950—Kittanning, Pennsylvania

Summer Picnic at Fred Deuschle's home (Maternal Grandparents)—
Kittanning, Pennsylvania

Lou's wife Susan's Family at the Robb Farm—
Huntingdon, Pennsylvania

Lou's Parents Fiftieth Wedding Anniversary—
1981—Franklin, Pennsylvania

Lou's wife Susan: Daughter, Bethany; Brother in Law, Duncan
and wife Nancy; Niece and Nephew, Allyson and Duncan
at the Robb Farm—Huntingdon, PA

Scotty's Family and Lou's Family on vacation at the beach—
Outer Banks, North Carolina

SELECTION 17: **JESUS IS ALWAYS THERE**

S (Scripture) Matthew 28:18-19: "Then Jesus came to them and said, 'All authority in heaven and on earth has been given to me. Therefore go and make disciples of all nations, baptizing them in the name of the Father and of the Son and of the Holy Spirit, and teaching them to obey everything I have commanded you. And surely I am with you always, to the very end of the age.'"

T (Thought/Think about it) Thank God that he is with me always to the end of the age.

O (Outline Priority) Because God is with me, I will go and make disciples for Jesus Christ. It is the priority of my life to share the good news. I have been blessed, so why not share what I know to be the ultimate truth? Jesus loves me and has the best plan for my life.

P (Prayer) I praise and express gratitude to God the Father, God the Son, and God the Holy Spirit for always being with me. Help me, Lord, I pray, to help others to know the good news of your eternal love, grace, and peace. I love you, Lord, and thank you for this blessed promise. Use me in your kingdom's work. Amen.

Stop and Take a Moment to Reflect: Have you placed Jesus Christ on the throne of your life, or are you in the way?

Suggested Reading: Matthew 28

SELECTION 18: **BE STRONG AND STAND FIRM**

S (Scripture) 1 Corinthians 16:13-14: "Be on your guard; stand firm in the faith; be courageous; be strong. Do everything in love."

T (Thought/Think about it) This is good advice from Paul to the Corinthians. These are good instructions that apply to me today.

O (Outline Priority) I need to be strong and stand firm in my faith.

P (Prayer) Loving God, my God, help me to be on guard, to be aware of those situations that would pull me away from you. Help me always to hold onto my faith in the Lord Jesus Christ, and help me to always share your love. The world as I know it needs men who are aware and steadfast in their belief of Jesus; men who are courageous in their witness and ability to stand up for what is true; men who are strong, committed Christians. Oh Lord, help me, I pray, to be one of those men. In thy name I pray. Amen.

Stop and Take a Moment to Reflect: In times of weakness, where do you find strength, courage, and faith?

Suggested Reading: 1 Corinthians 16:5-18

SELECTION 19: **KEEP THE SABBATH**

S (Scripture) Exodus 20:8: "Remember the Sabbath day by keeping it holy."

T (Thought/Think about it) If the Sabbath was important enough to be included in the Ten Commandments, it is important enough for me to honor it and keep it holy.

O (Outline Priority) I will do my best to keep Sunday a day of rest, a day of worship, and a day of spiritual reflection.

P (Prayer) Lord Jesus, thank you for Sunday. Thank you for all the lessons I have been taught from wonderful pastors, teachers, and Christian friends who have encouraged and blessed my life. Amen.

Stop and Take a Moment to Reflect: What have I done to make Sunday a holy day?

Suggested Reading: Exodus 20

SELECTION 20: **SELF-EXAMINATION**

S (Scripture) 1 Corinthians 11:28: "A man ought to examine himself before he eats of the bread and drinks of the cup."

T (Thought/Think about it) Self-examination would have me admit my sins and shortcomings. Upon self-examination, I know my need for grace, forgiveness, and compassion. I fall short in so many ways.

O (Outline Priority) I am a sinner who stands in need of Jesus Christ, the Savior of the world.

P (Prayer) My Lord and my God, oh how I love you and your perfect plan for my life. You paid the price. There is no way I could earn my salvation; it came from your grace. That thought overwhelms me. My fellowship is restored because of your sacrificial death and resurrection. Thank you, Lord, for saving my soul. Amen.

Stop and Take a Moment to Reflect: Take time today for some self-examination, a spiritual checkup.

Suggested Reading: 1 Corinthians 11:17-34

SELECTION 21: **DO NOT FOLLOW THE CROWD**

S (Scripture) Exodus 23:2: "Do not follow the crowd in doing wrong."

T (Thought/Think about it) It is common practice in today's society to follow the crowd; after all, "Everyone's doing it!" This verse is powerful with great implications and impact for the contemporary generation.

O (Outline Priority) I will follow the leading of the Holy Spirit. As a Christian, I am not to follow the crowd but rather to seek and do the work of the Lord.

P (Prayer) Lord Jesus, thank you for keeping me in your will and plan for my life. Help me, I pray, to stay on the straight and narrow path. Lord, you and I know that Satan would like to derail me at any moment, but with your guidance, leading, and power that will not happen. In your name I pray. Amen.

Stop and Take a Moment to Reflect: When it is popular to do the wrong thing, who keeps you from participating?

Suggested Reading: Exodus 23:1-9

SELECTION 22: **READ THE WORD, GET BLESSED**

S (Scripture) Revelation 1:3: "Blessed is the one who reads the words of this prophecy, and blessed are those who hear it and take to heart what is written in it, because the time is near."

T (Thought/Think about it) I am blessed to read these words recorded by John. This book can be troubling to those who waver in their personal relationship with the Lord. This book brings hope to me because my faith is secure not in anything I have done but in what the Lord has done for me.

O (Outline Priority) I will continue to walk in the path of my Lord Jesus Christ. I look forward to his coming. He will protect and guide me and will prevail over evil.

P (Prayer) Praise God for his wonderful plan, which is so clear to me. I praise the Father. I praise the Son. I praise the Holy Spirit. I praise the three-in-one. Lord Jesus, I look forward to your triumphant and glorious return. Amen.

Stop and Take a Moment to Reflect: I may not understand every word in the Holy Scriptures, but I know my life will be blessed for reading the Word. Do you take joy in reading God's Word?

Suggested Reading: Revelation 1:1-8

SELECTION 23: **I CAN KNOW I HAVE ETERNAL LIFE**

S (Scripture) 1 John 5:11-13: "And this is the testimony: God has given us eternal life, and this life is in his Son. Whoever has the Son has life; whoever does not have the Son of God does not have life. I write these things to you who believe in the name of the Son of God so that you may know that you have eternal life."

T (Thought/Think about it) I love these three verses. I know without a shadow of doubt that I have eternal life.

O (Outline Priority) Jesus is my Savior. Jesus is my number one priority. I believe in the life, death, and resurrection of Jesus. I know that my eternity is certain and secure.

P (Prayer) I praise you, my Lord, my Savior, my Jesus. Thank you for knocking at my heart's door. I accepted you at a young age and asked you to come into my heart. You, dear Jesus, are the only way. I know and accept your forgiving grace. Thank you, God the Father, for loving me so much that you sent your Son to die for my sins. I praise and thank you, Holy Spirit, for guiding, directing, and comforting me in my need. Praise to you Father, Son, and Holy Spirit. Amen.

Stop and Take a Moment to Reflect: Do you know without a shadow of a doubt that you have eternal life? I encourage you to give your life completely to the love, grace, and care of Jesus. I encourage you to pray this simple prayer: "Lord Jesus, I know I am not perfect; I have sinned and fallen short of your glory. I ask you to forgive my sins and come into my heart today. I thank you and praise your name, Father, Son, and Holy Spirit, that I can know I have eternal life. Amen."

Suggested Reading: 1 John 5

SELECTION 24: **MY WITNESS**

S (Scripture) Acts 1:8: "But you will receive power when the Holy Spirit comes on you; and you will be my witnesses in Jerusalem, and in all Judea and Samaria, and to the ends of the earth."

T (Thought/Think about it) Jesus promised the disciples that they would have power to witness after they received the Holy Spirit.

O (Outline Priority) I need to be aware of and look for opportunities to witness for my Lord and Savior, Jesus.

P (Prayer) Lord Jesus, today I pray that I am able to touch someone in some way with your love, grace, power, and salvation. Help me to be the witness you have prepared me to be. I ask this in your holy name. Amen.

Stop and Take a Moment to Reflect: Have you witnessed to anyone lately?

Suggested Reading: Acts 1:1-11

SELECTION 25: **THE CARDINAL**

S (Scripture) Psalm 86:17: "Give me a sign of your goodness, that my enemies may see it and be put to shame, for you, O LORD, have helped me and comforted me."

T (Thought/Think about it) David asked for a sign when he was in deep trouble. I asked for a sign, and God provided the cardinal.

O (Outline Priority) The cardinal frequently appears at the precise moment that I need it the most. Isn't that interesting?

P (Prayer) Lord, you have given me so much through my family and friends, your holy Word, prayer, and the joy of each day. But when I needed a direct word from you, I asked for a cardinal to appear, and it did! I love you, Lord of my life. Amen.

Stop and Take a Moment to Reflect: Have you taken the time to appreciate God's love, wonder, and power through his creation?

Psalm 19:1-4:

> The heavens declare the glory of God;
> the skies proclaim the work of his hands.
> Day after day they pour forth speech;
> night after night they reveal knowledge.
> They have no speech, they use no words;
> no sound is heard from them.

Yet their voice goes out into all the earth,
their words to the ends of the world.
In the heavens God has pitched a tent for the sun.

Suggested Reading: Psalm 86

SELECTION 26: **HOPE IN JESUS**

S (Scripture) 1 Thessalonians 4:13-14: "Brothers, we do not want you to be ignorant about those who fall asleep, or to grieve like the rest of men, who have no hope. We believe that Jesus died and rose again and so we believe that God will bring with Jesus those who have fallen asleep in him."

T (Thought/Think about it) As I walk through this life one day at a time, may my life, testimony, and future rest secure in the knowledge that my hope is in the death and resurrection of Jesus Christ.

O (Outline Priority) My hope is in Jesus Christ, period.

P (Prayer) Thank you, Jesus, for saving me from a world that lacks hope. Be with those who do not know you or the power of your resurrection. May I share the good news of these verses with those who have little or no hope. Thank you, Lord, for the numerous times these words have brought comfort and hope to me and those I love in our times of need. Amen.

Stop and Take a Moment to Reflect: When all seems hopeless, where do you turn? I encourage you to turn your life and all that it encompasses to the love, grace, and care of Jesus.

Suggested Reading: 1 Thessalonians 4:13-18

SELECTION 27: **LOVE, THE GREATEST OF THESE**

S (Scripture) 1 Corinthians 13:13: "And now these three remain: faith, hope, and love. But the greatest of these is love."

T (Thought/Think about it) This verse, part of the love chapter in the Bible and my daughter Bethany's favorite Scripture, has been shared at many wedding ceremonies. Unfortunately, too many of those weddings have resulted in separation, conflict, and divorce. This verse addresses the necessity of faith, hope, and love in the life of the believer.

O (Outline Priority) My faith, hope, and love originate in the life, death, and resurrection of Jesus, the Savior of the world.

P (Prayer) Lord Jesus, I praise your holy name for your supreme gift of love expressed on the cross for the sins of the world. My faith, hope, and indeed my love are a direct result of your sacrifice. I know how difficult it can be to express love in trying situations. Help me, Lord, to be more faithful, more hopeful, and more loving each day.

Stop and Take a Moment to Reflect: Is your faith, hope, and love secure in the life, death, and resurrection of Jesus the Savior?

Suggested Reading: 1 Corinthians 13

SELECTION 28: **GIFT OF GOD**

S (Scripture) Ephesians 2:8-9: "By grace you have been saved through faith; and that not of yourselves, it is the gift of God; not as result of works that no one should boast."

T (Thought/Think about it) There is no way I could earn my salvation; it is a gift from God.

O (Outline Priority) I know how blessed I am to have the love, grace, and forgiveness that comes freely when I place my complete trust and faith in Jesus the Christ.

P (Prayer) Lord Jesus, thank you for saving my soul and guiding my life each step of the way, in spite of myself. Help me, I pray, to seek your will daily as I face the challenges, temptations, and joys of life. In your blessed name I pray. Amen.

Stop and Take a Moment to Reflect: Isn't it amazing that you cannot earn your way into heaven? It is a free gift. When I receive a gift, it means nothing unless I open it and use it in my life. Have you released your life completely to the love, grace, and care of the Father?

Suggested Reading: Ephesians 2:1-10

SELECTION 29: **WHO IS JESUS?**

S (Scripture) Matthew 16:13-15: "When Jesus came to the region of Caesarea Philippi, he asked his disciples, 'Who do people say the Son of Man is?' They replied, 'Some say John the Baptist; others say Elijah; and still others, Jeremiah or one of the prophets.' 'But what about you?' he asked. 'Who do you say I am?'"

T (Thought/Think about it) Jesus was speaking directly to me in the verses from Matthew 16. "Lou, who do you say I am?"

O (Outline Priority) Jesus, you are the light of the world. You are the bright morning star. You are the Savior of my life.

P (Prayer) Lord Jesus, I know who you are because you have been a part of my life since I opened the door of my heart as a child for your entrance. I love, worship, obey, and praise your holy name. Amen.

Stop and Take a Moment to Reflect: Who do you say Jesus is?

Suggested Reading: Matthew 16:13-20

SELECTION 30: **HAVE FAITH: GOD WILL TAKE CARE OF YOU**

S (Scripture) Mark 4:40: "He said to his disciples, 'Why are you so afraid? Do you still have no faith?'"

T (Thought/Think about it) The disciples were afraid that they would drown. Jesus calmed the wind and the waves and asked the disciples, "Why are you afraid? Do you still have no faith?"

O (Outline Priority) The storms of life will come. Jesus is able. Jesus is all-knowing. Jesus is all-powerful. Jesus is all-time present. Jesus will see us through the tough times of our lives if we place our faith and trust in Him. I choose to trust my Lord Jesus in every phase of my life.

P (Prayer) Lord Jesus, thank you for seeing me through the storms of my life. Thank you for the calm and peace only you can provide. When I'm in a difficult situation, I will trust you and you alone to deliver me. I also trust you completely for my family and friends. Thank you, Lord, and praise your holy name. Amen.

Stop and Take a Moment to Reflect: When you go through the deep waters of life, in whom do you place your trust?

Suggested Reading: Mark 4:35-41

SELECTION 31: **A PERFECT PRAYER**

S (Scripture) Numbers 6:24-26: "The LORD bless you and keep you; the LORD make his face shine upon you and be gracious to you; the LORD turn his face toward you and give you peace."

T (Thought/Think about it) What a prayer! What a blessing!

O (Outline Priority) This is the blessing I desire for my family and friends.

P (Prayer) Oh Lord God, this is the perfect prayer I desire each day. Thank you, Lord, for your blessing, for your keeping, for shining your light in my life, for your graciousness, and for the peace that comes only through your grace. Amen.

Stop and Take a Moment to Reflect: Do you trust the Lord completely?

Suggested Reading: Numbers 6:22-27

FINAL THOUGHT

It is my desire to know you for eternity, not just on this earth. If you are a family member, treasured friend, colleague, or a friend-to-be, I pray that you have gained godly wisdom from these passages.

As an athlete needs to practice, refine, and condition his skills, a Christian needs the daily regimen of prayer, Bible reading, and fellowship to remain committed to the task God has prepared in advance for him or her to complete. I have intentionally kept the devotional practical and to the point in the hope that each selection will touch, motivate, and encourage each of you to greater levels of Christian maturation.

For further growth in your faith journey, I recommend my favorite books and pamphlets listed on the "For Further Reading" page.

Remember to STOP in your daily walk and read the good news.

FOR FURTHER READING

Life Application Study Bible, New International Version, Published by Zondervan, Grand Rapids, Michigan

The Billy Graham Christian Worker's Handbook, World Wide Publishers Minneapolis, Minnesota

Growing Strong in the Seasons of Life, Charles R. Swindoll, Multnomah Press, Portland, Oregon

God's Inspirational Promise Book, Max Lucado, Word Publishing, Inc. Dallas, Texas

Life is Like That, Glenn "Tex" Evans, Appalachia Service Project, Inc. Johnson City, Tennessee

Four Spiritual Laws, Bill Bright, Campus Crusade for Christ International, Arrowhead Springs, San Bernardino, California

Hope for Each Day, Billy Graham, J. Countryman Publishers

90 Minutes in Heaven: A True Story of Death & Life, Don Piper, Baker Publishing

Heaven is for Real, Todd Burpo, Thomas Nelson Publishing

Experiencing God Day by Day, Henry T. Blackaby and Richard Blackaby, B & H Publishing, Nashville, Tennessee

My Utmost for His Highest, Oswald Chambers, Discovery House Publishers, Grand Rapids Michigan

Living with Confidence in a Chaotic World, Dr. David Jeremiah, Thomas Nelson Publishing

Crazy Love, Francis Chan, Published by David C. Cook, Colorado Springs, CO

"Our Daily Bread" Devotional, RBC Ministries Grand Rapids, MI

"The Upper Room" Devotional, Upper Room Ministries, Nashville, TN

CPSIA information can be obtained at www.ICGtesting.com
Printed in the USA
BVOW011853150512

290306BV00005B/1/P